Seasons

Fall

Siân Smith

Heinemann Library
Chicago, Illinois

Editorial: Rebecca Rissman, Charlotte Guillain, and Siân Smith
Picture research: Elizabeth Alexander and Sally Claxton
Designed by Joanna Hinton-Malivoire
Printed in China

13 12 11
10 9 8 7 6 5 4 3 2 1

ISBN-13: 978-1-4329-5779-7 (saddle-stitch)

Library of Congress Cataloging-in-Publication Data
Cataloging-in-Publication data is available at the Library of Congress.

Acknowledgments
The author and publisher are grateful to the following for permission to reproduce copyright material:
©Alamy pp.**10, 11** (Blend Images), **20** (David Norton), **9** (Judy Freilicher), **14**, **23 bottom** (Neil Dangerfield), **8** (Phill Lister), **16** (Renee Morris), **21** (Silksatsunrise Photography); ©Corbis pp.**22** (Craig Tuttle), **04 br** (Image100), **17** (Tetra Images), **04 tl** (Zefa/Roman Flury); ©GAP Photos pp.**18, 23 top** (Fiona Lea); ©Getty Images pp.**04 tr** (Floria Werner), **5** (Philippe Renault); ©iStockphoto.com pp.**6, 23 middle** (Bojan Tezak), **04 bl** (Inga Ivanova); ©Photodisc p.**12** (Photolink); ©Photolibrary pp.**13** (Chad Ehlers), **15** (J-Charles Gerard/Photononstop); ©Punchstock p.**7** (Brand X Pictures/Morey Milbradt); ©Shutterstock p.**19** (Vakhrushev Pavel).

Cover photograph of maple tree reproduced with permission of ©Shutterstock (Tatiana Grozetskaya). Back cover photograph reproduced with permission of ©Photodisc (Photolink).

Every effort has been made to contact copyright holders of any material reproduced in this book. Any omissions will be rectified in subsequent printings if notice is given to the publisher.

006125/042011

Contents

What Is Fall?

spring

summer

fall

winter

There are four seasons every year.

Fall is one of the four seasons.

When Is Fall?

spring

summer

winter

fall

The four seasons follow a pattern.

Fall comes after summer.

The Weather in Fall

It can be cooler in fall.

It can be foggy in fall.

What Can We See in Fall?

In fall we can see people in sweaters.

In fall we can see people in coats.

In fall we can see colored leaves on trees.

In fall we can see colored leaves on the ground.

In fall we can see seeds.

In fall we can see fruits
and vegetables.

In fall we can see berries.

In fall we can see pumpkins.

In fall we can see bonfires.

In fall we can see fireworks.

In fall we can see animals carrying food.

In fall we can see birds flying away.

Which Season Comes Next?

Which season comes after fall?

Picture Glossary

 **bonfire** outdoor fire

 **pattern** happening in the same order

 **seed** plants make seeds. Seeds grow into new plants.

Index

Note to Parents and Teachers
Before reading
Explain to children that there are four seasons every year: winter, spring, summer and fall.
Tell children that the seasons follow a pattern, or sequence. Write the four seasons on the
board and draw arrows showing their order. Show children that fall comes after summer.
Ask them what their favorite fall activities are.

After reading
Make a garland of leaves. You will need enough leaves from different trees for each child
to have one leaf; paper, pencils, crayons, scissors, and a long piece of string. Tell children to
select a leaf from your collection and to draw it on a piece of paper with a thick stem. They
should then mark the veins and cut out their leaf.
Fold the stem in half and attach it to the string. Suspend the string of leaves across
the classroom.